Fantagraphics Books, 7563 Lake City Way NE, Seattle, Washington 98115 | EDITED AND DESIGNED BY Jonathan Barli SUPERVISING EDITOR: Gary Groth ASSOCIATE PUBLISHER: Eric Reynolds PUBLISHER: Gary Groth | CORK HIGH AND BOTTLE DEEP is copyright © 2014 Fantagraphics Books. All rights reserved. Permission to reproduce material must be obtained from the publisher. | Thanks to Ger Apeldoorn and Paul Tumey for contributing artwork for this volume. | Fantagraphics would like to thank: Karen Green, Secret Headquarters, Eduardo Takeo "Lizarkeo" Igarashi, John DiBello, Ted Haycraft, Andy Koopmans, Juan Manuel Domínguez, Paul van Dijken, Nick Capetillo, Randall Bethune, Kevin Czapiewski, Thomas Eykemans, Christian Schremser, Thomas Zimmermann, Kurt Sayenga, Anne Lise Rostgaard Schmidt, Coco and Eddie Gorodetsky, Big Planet Comics, Nevdon Jamgochian, Dan Evans III, Scott Fritsch-Hammes, Black Hook Press of Japan, Mungo van Krimpen-Hall, Philip Nel, Jason Aaron Wong, Vanessa Palacios, and Mathieu Doublet. | To receive a free full-color catalog of comics, graphic novels, prose novels, and other fine works of artistry including VIP: THE MAD WORLD OF VIRGIL PARTCH, call 1-800-657-1100, or visit www.fantagraphics. com. You may order books at our web site or by phone. | ISBN: 978-1-60699-716-1 | First Fantagraphics printing: June 2014 | Printed in China

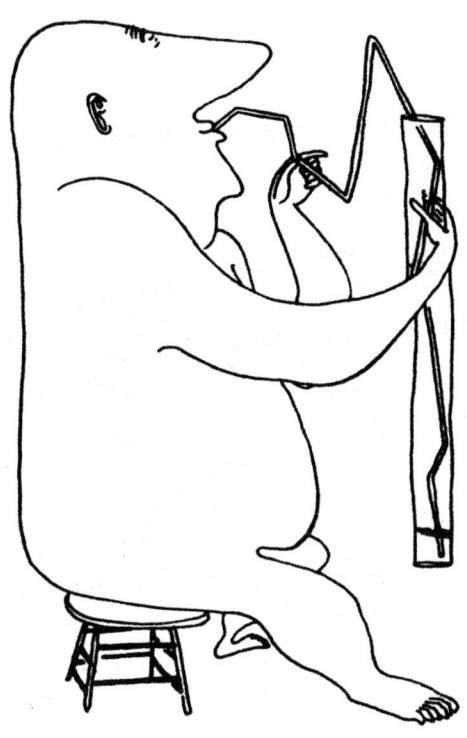

The Author recommends that you have a drink before absorbing all this knowledge.

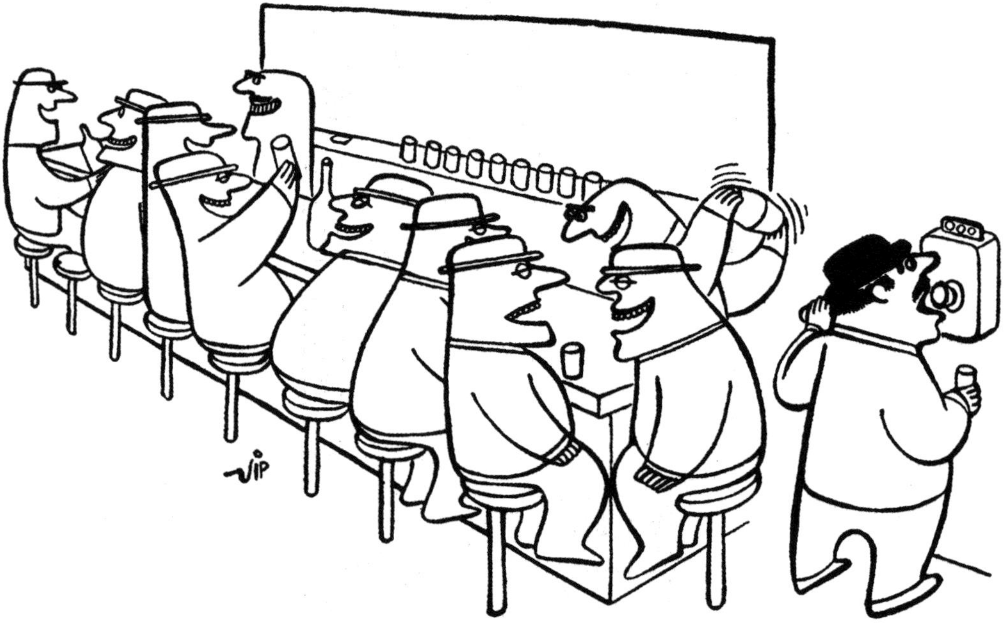
VIP

"Guess where I am, dear."

CORK HIGH
AND
BOTTLE DEEP

*Amidst the stormy seas of booze, with
your faithful skipper, the mad Vipper*

Cartoons by

VIRGIL  PARTCH

Edited by JONATHAN BARLI

FANTAGRAPHICS BOOKS — SEATTLE

"It's a safety belt."

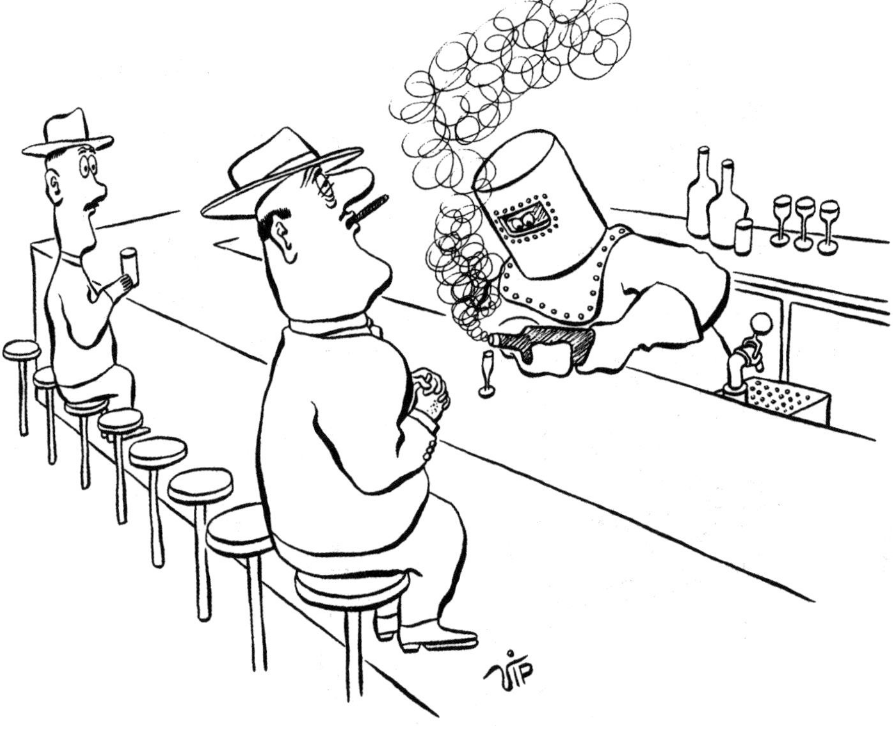
VIP

"Name your poison."

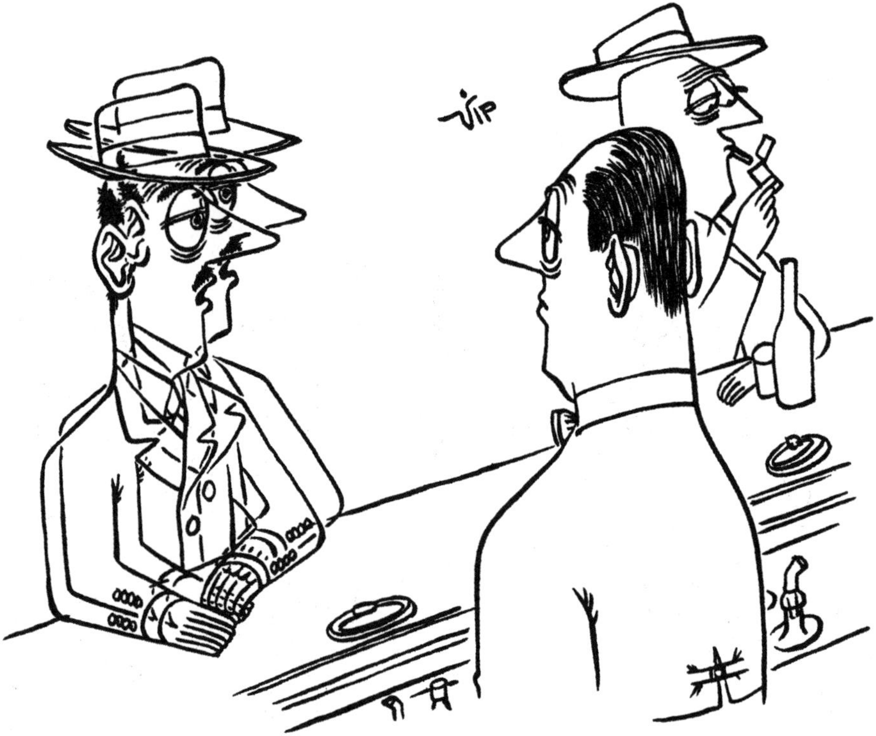
VIP

"Double Martini"

"A bourbon and water ... double!"

"I said <u>straight</u> bourbon."

"Let's see ... what was I drinking to forget?"

Straight.

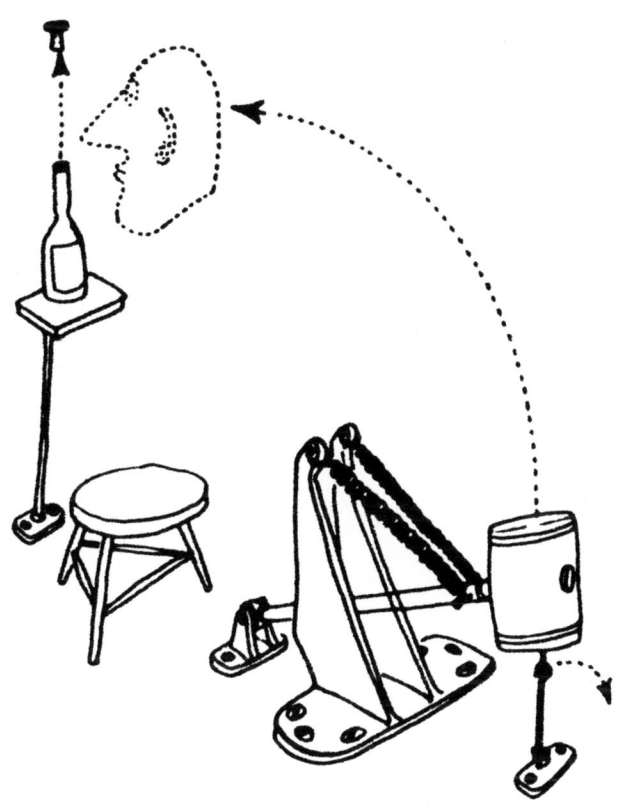

"No chaser for me, thanks."

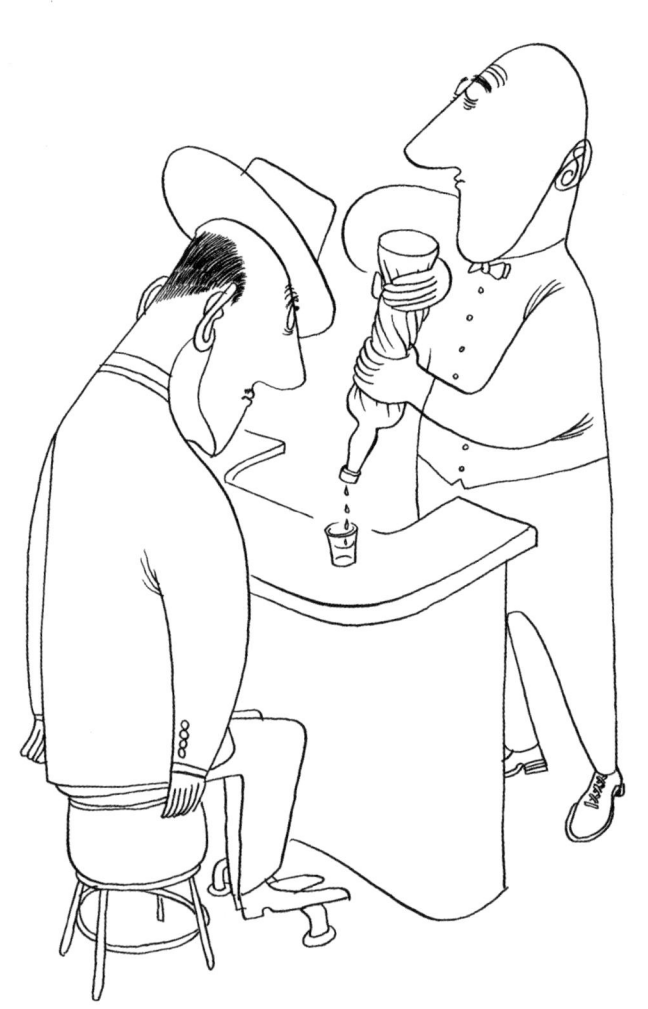

"On second thought I __will__ have that water chaser."

"He's right ... it says, 'Not for internal use.'"

"Put a head on mine, please."

"Oh, yeh! If today's the nineteenth, I'll eat my hat."

"It's the only way I can keep in shape."

"He's trying to stay off the bottle."

"We have more Scotch than we know what to do with."

"It may not be ten years old, but you can't deny it's Scotch."

"Why didn't you wait till I got my drink before you told him your troubles?"

"Not __that__ button."

"Two more dry Martinis. Leave out the olives this time."

"Stop worrying. You never eat the olives, anyway."

"It's some woman."

Love that stuff!

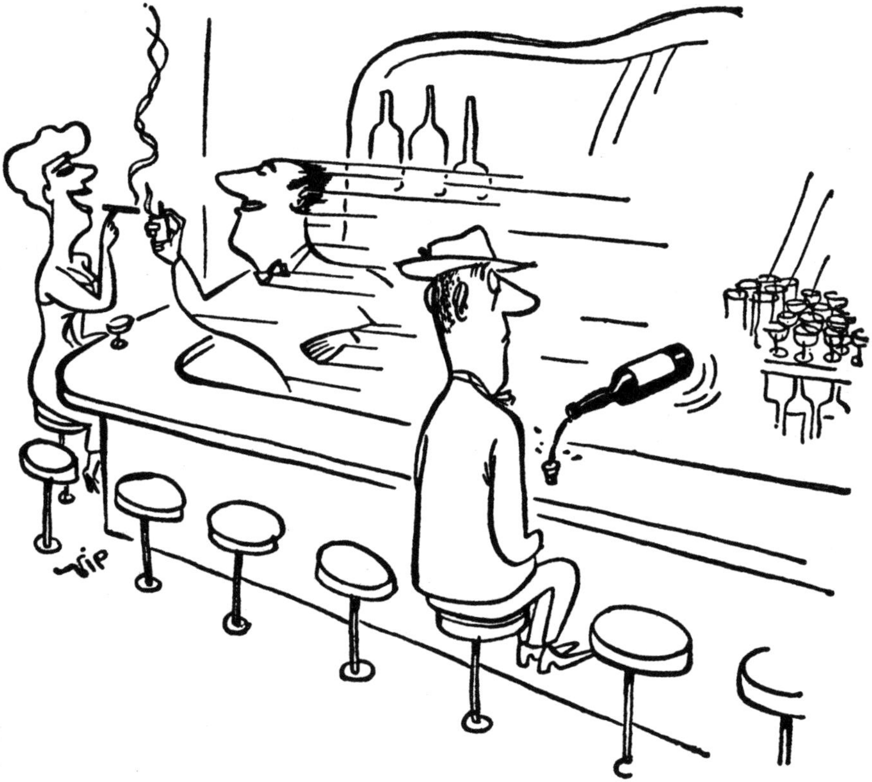

Tip

"Thanks."

"Would you mind moving your things, Madame?"

"We've been wondering why you're not in uniform."

"Better not pull me up for an hour or so."

"Yes ... yes, ma'am ... I'll see if he's still here."

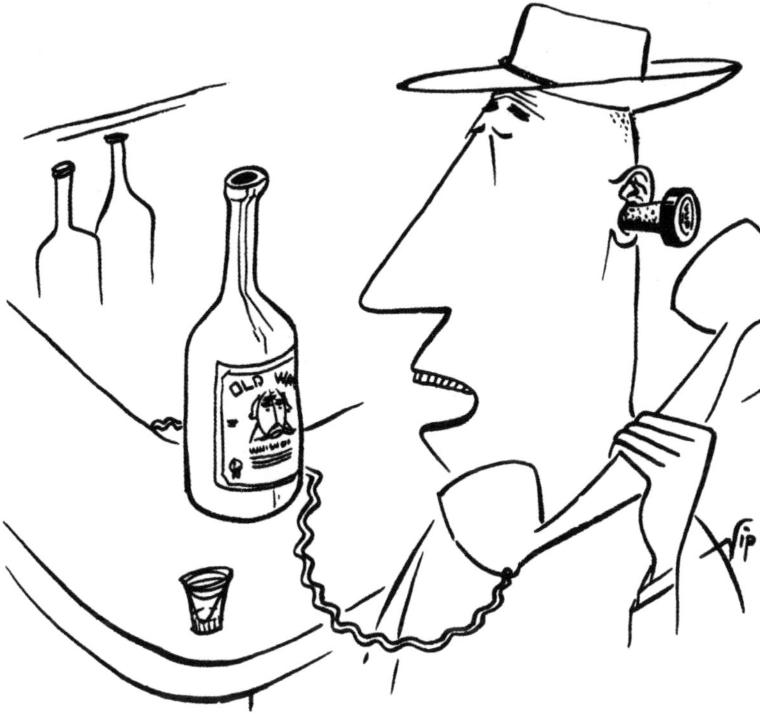
OLD

"Speak up, dear. What is it?"

"Well, there goes Bodki — late for dinner again."

"I don't care if you believe it or not — I tell you I can't tear myself away."

"Well ... did she say you could stay out?"

"The bartender's my husband."

"Damn these reformed drunks!"

"He never touches the stuff."

"He wants to know what's in it — his headache's completely disappeared."

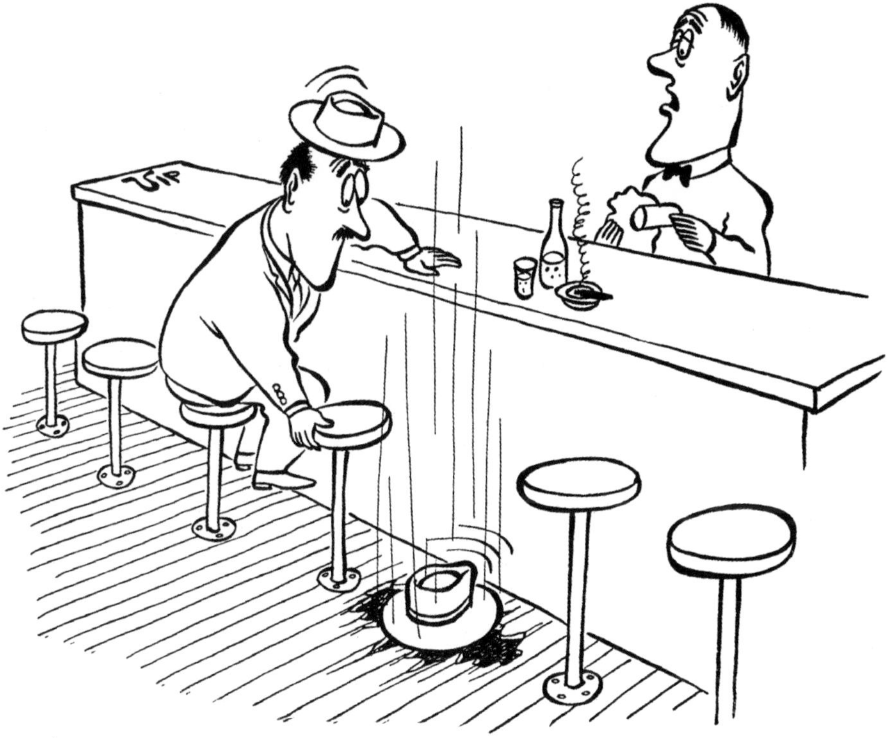
Sip

"Termites."

"What say we dive into a couple of tall ones?"

"Unusually small crowd for a Saturday night."

"A short beer."

"I'll have to ask to see your driver's license."

"I was a boxer once myself."

"He said to stop him if we'd heard it before."

"Never drink on an empty stomach."

"Oh, him? He sometimes gets mean when he drinks."

"You wouldn't hit a guy with glasses on, would you?"

"You'll do what to him, chum?"

"*That's a sweet uppercut you have there.*"

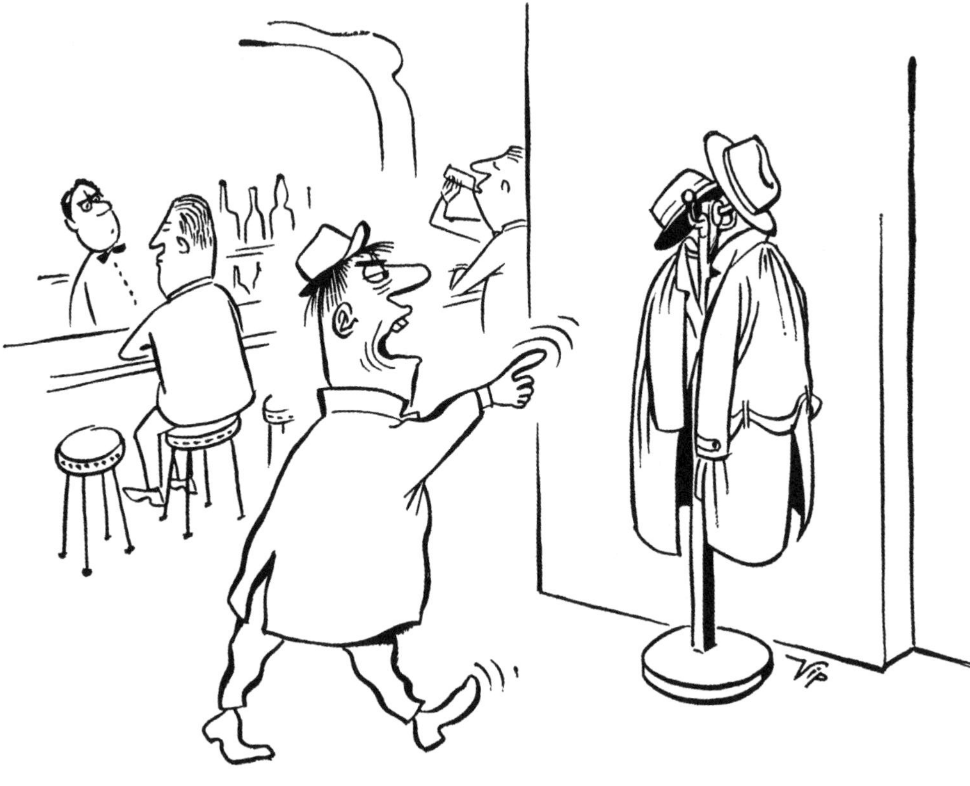
Vip

"Break it up!"

"Let's leave Al out this next round."

"Thanks, no. I'd rather stand."

"Go on, feel his grip."

"You've had enough!"

"Please! You two go outside."

A touching rescue scene.

"Down the hall. You can't miss it."

"One thing about old Ed — he never drinks without eating."

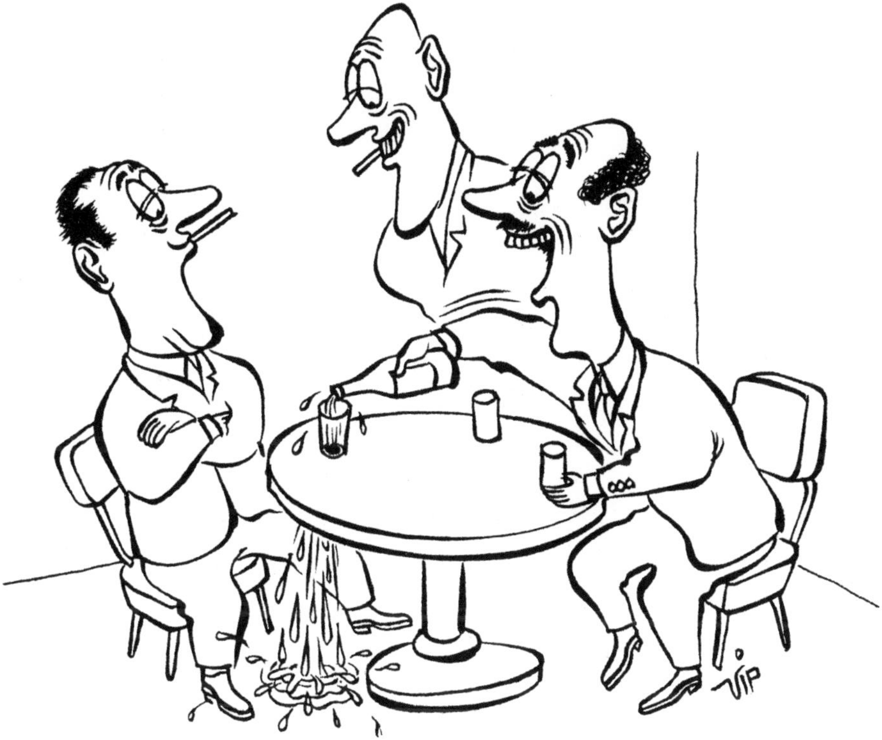
VIP

"Say when!"

"Definitely stir-crazy."

"Could you bring another straw when you have a moment?"

"Gosh, Ed's folded up already."

"Never knows when to quit, does he?"

"No, thanks — keeps me awake."

"I've been wondering why that phone was so low."

"Now there goes a real gent."

"Gasoline and alcohol don't mix, young man!"

"These two are taken."

"But see, sir. Ten Martinis at sixty cents each is ..."

"But I tried reasoning with him."

"I'm looking for my husband."

"Have I kept you waiting very long, dear?"

"Not so loud ... bouncer right behind you."

"Never <u>did</u> have a head for the hard stuff."

"Easy, Ed. He's the only guy with any dough."

"Gad! What follow-through."

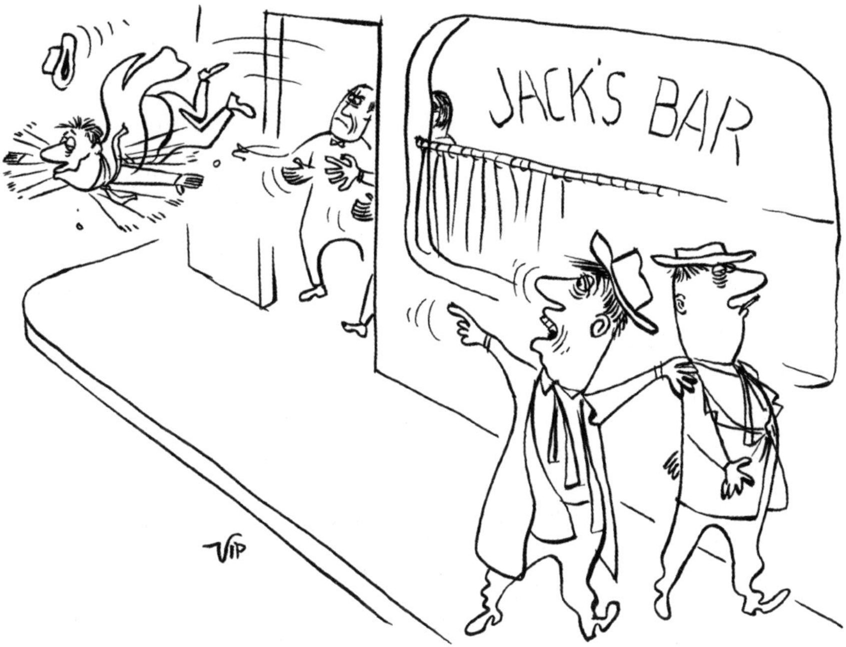
JACK'S BAR
VIP

"Hey, look — Al can fly."

"Hold it, fellows. I can stay out a little longer after all."

"Honey, I want you to meet a fellow horse-lover."

"Sure it's cold, but if you insist on going out and getting plastered ..."

*"OK ... OK. You have a very cute little button nose ...
which is rather red, I might add."*

"Ward, you've been drinking."

"Well, just sober up some other place!"

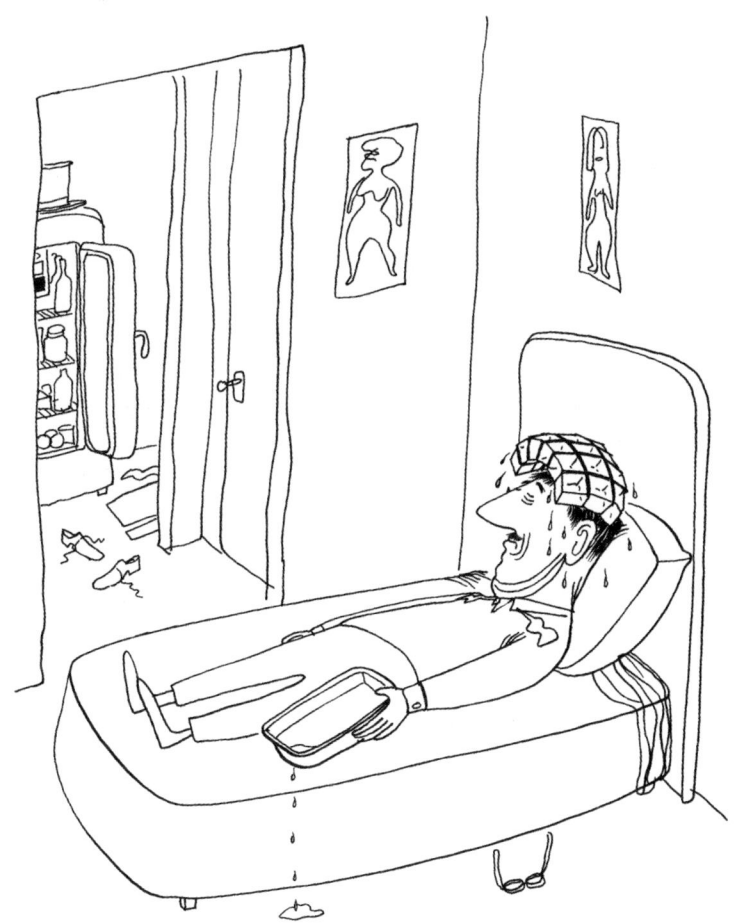

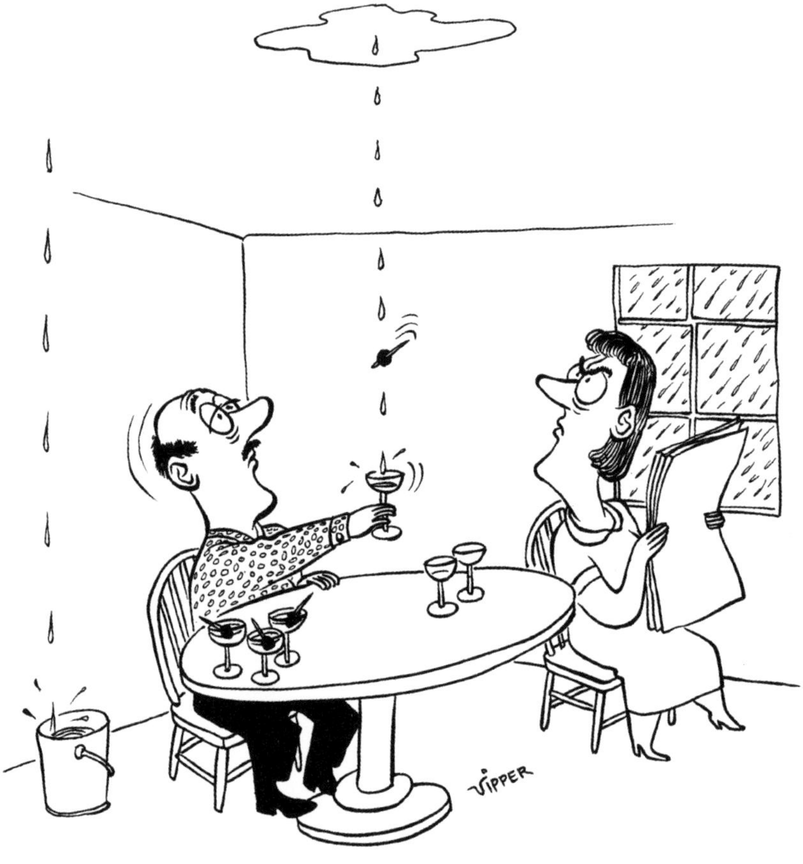
VIPPER

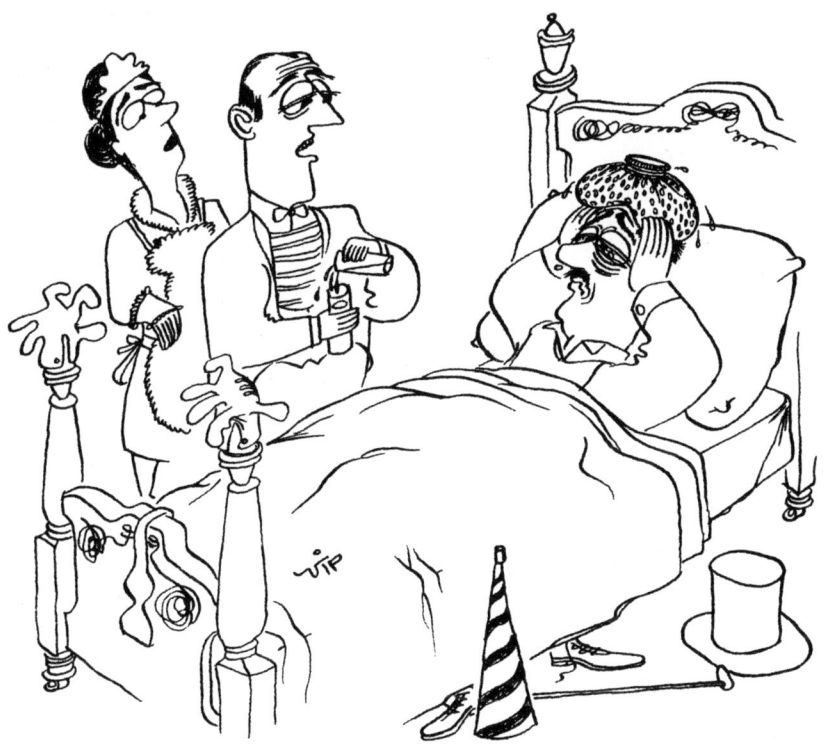

"But, sir, we can't help you unless you have the _desire_ to live."

"Now __that's__ what I call a __real__ pick-me-up!"

"Idiot! I didn't say to get me a pick-up. I said a pick-me-up."

"It's not <u>supposed</u> to be a pick-me-up. It's poison."

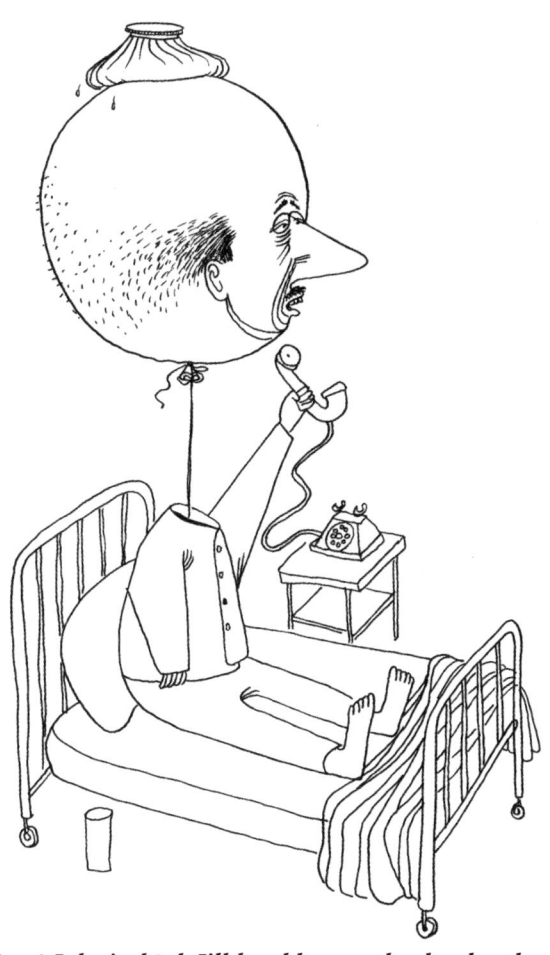

"Hello, Sam? I don't think I'll be able to make that luncheon date."

"Friend ... the game is __not__ over."

"I believe I left my topcoat here last night."

THE HANGOVER...

The Please-No-Sudden-Noises Hangover

The Laughing-on-the-Outside-
Crying-on-the-Inside Hangover

The Shakes Hangover

The Chicken-Little Hangover

The Whole-Ghastly-Room-Is-Spinning Hangover

The I-Refuse-to-Remember Hangover

The How-Can-I-Ever-Face-Them Hangover

The Pull-Those-Goddam-Blinds Hangover

The Sawing-Woman-in-Half Hangover

The Nine-Iron Hangover

The Ground-Zero Hangover

The I-Must-Have-Gone-Ten-Fast-Rounds Hangover

The Grassy-Tongue Hangover

The Don't-You-Hear-It-Too? Hangover

The Nothing-Seems-Real Hangover

The I'm-All-Right-as-Long-as-I-Don't-Bend-Over Hangover

The Rosy-Outlook Hangover

THIRSTY-BEDOUIN HANGOVER

*Common early in drinking career after a big binge; hardly worth
mentioning to the real lush. Craving for gallons of ice water was
long explained by doctors as result of alcohol drying out body tissues.
Bosh! The desert mirage is a morning reality; Bedouin midget filters
water through sand, producing beer. When he gets tipsy, so are you.*

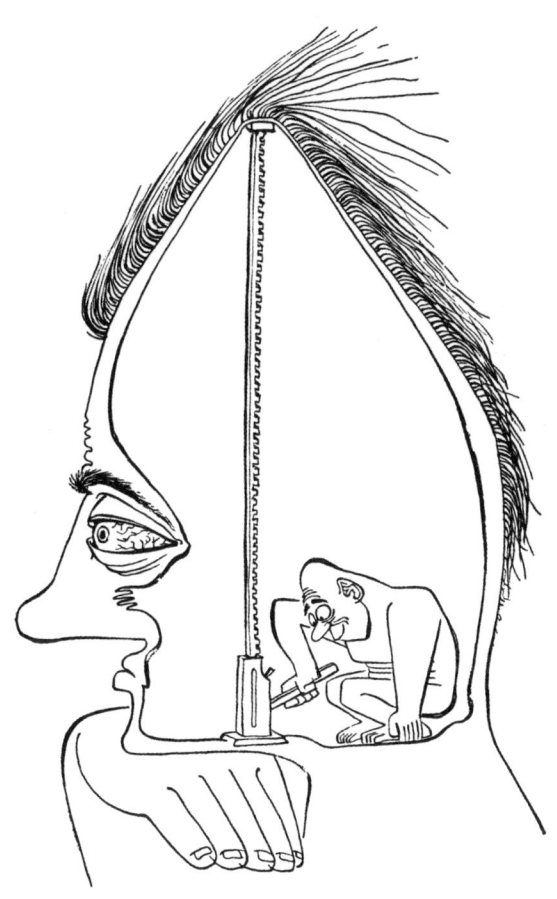

MECHANICAL EXPANDING-THROB TYPE

Now we're getting somewhere; serious drinkers will listen to complaint of this nature, particularly if it has accompanying shrill train-whistle effects. Diagnosed in medical circles as constriction of brain's blood vessels, this really comes from prankish Turk raising heavy-duty truck jack. Easily remedied by stepping off high building.

REVOLVING OLD-OVERCOAT TONGUE

Could have been something you ate, providing you go around gorging on stewed seagull, toadstools, or kalsomine. Can also be caused by cheap wines, boilermakers, or hair tonics in quantity. Often has no connection with drinking at all but is merely symptomatic of destroyed metabolism, ruptured liver, malfunctioning kidneys, and gallstones.

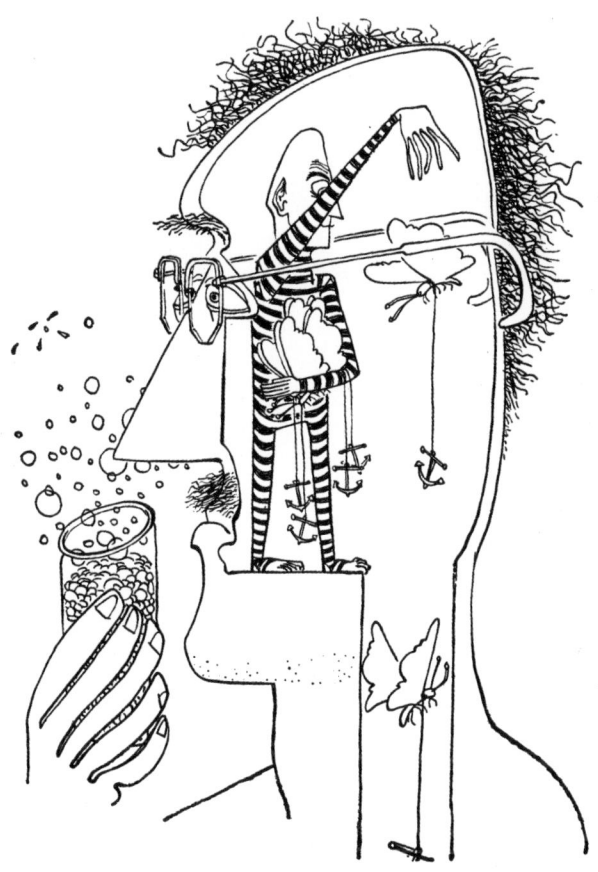

ANCHORED BUTTERFLY PHENOMENON

Popular with nervous, imaginative types. Also anybody else who drinks two quarts a day. If you haven't had 'em, you've probably heard mild-hangover man at bar in the morning, saying "Oh, these guys with the whips-and-jingles imagine most of that ———" just before jittery man murders him with bartender's baseball bat. With luck, victims strangle before noon.

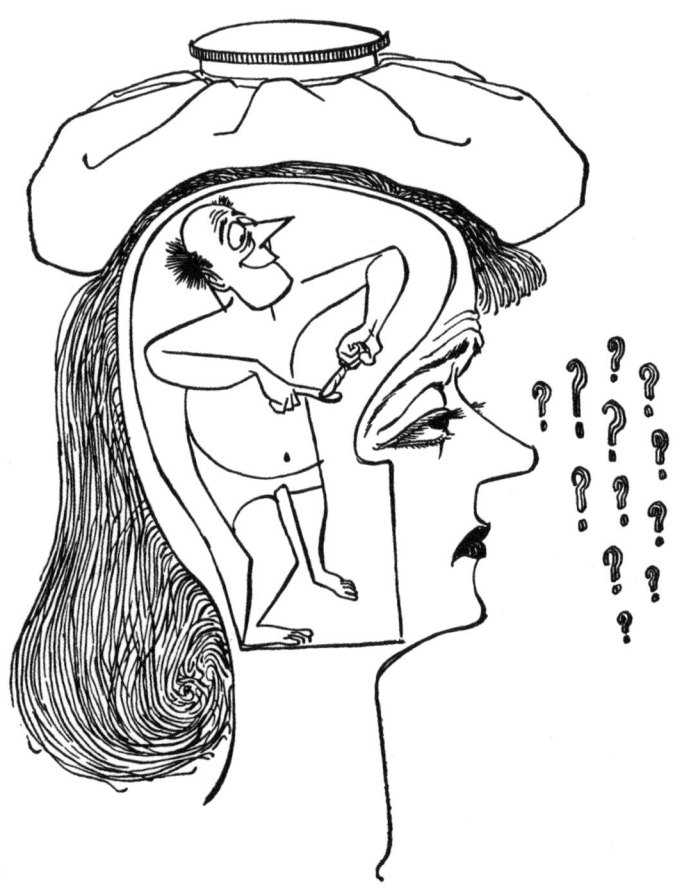

CONSCIENCE-STRICKEN *or* **"I'LL HATE MYSELF IN THE MORNING."**

Laughable old saying which comes true. Nice girl unsure just how much self-hating to administer. She'll find out; will avoid at least two men who were at the party until she gets a line on what happened after that sixth Daiquiri. Also in the novice class; experienced drinkers never try to remember.

EYEBALL SONATA or BOINGITIS OBBLIGATO

*Nothing worse than temporary blindness, becoming permanent in very few
cases since Prohibition. Greatest sufferers are music-lovers who become
self-conscious about off-key boing! chords given out at regular intervals.
Yale Clinic believes 190-proof alcohol and bitters will drown the harpist.
Poppycock! How many gin mills were they ever thrown out of?*

DESIRE FOR DEATH or WOW! TYPE HANGOVER

Rarely fatal; not really painful, either, if you have a detachable head. This interesting affliction has rather humorous aspects in that the victim usually says, "My head's splitting!" Is nonplussed when it does. Aspirin tablets will not dissolve; cyanide is occasionally effective. Little man is descendant of John Henry That Steel-Drivin' Man, comes out of jukeboxes that play hillbilly tunes. Hole in head eventually relieves internal pressure, thus partly ending the pain.

GOD! IS THAT ME? or HALLUCINATION CASE

This may or may not be serious depending on whether or not you consider delirium tremens and broken legs serious. The little man (composed largely of ectoplasm and discarded lemon peels out of Martinis) will either go away within 24 hours or at least put on some clothes. Then again, in 76.8 cases reported to the Partch Foundation, the dame simply never before had looked in a mirror this early in the morning. Now she knows what her husband has known for years.

... AND SOME CURES

The Water Cure

The Black Coffee Approach

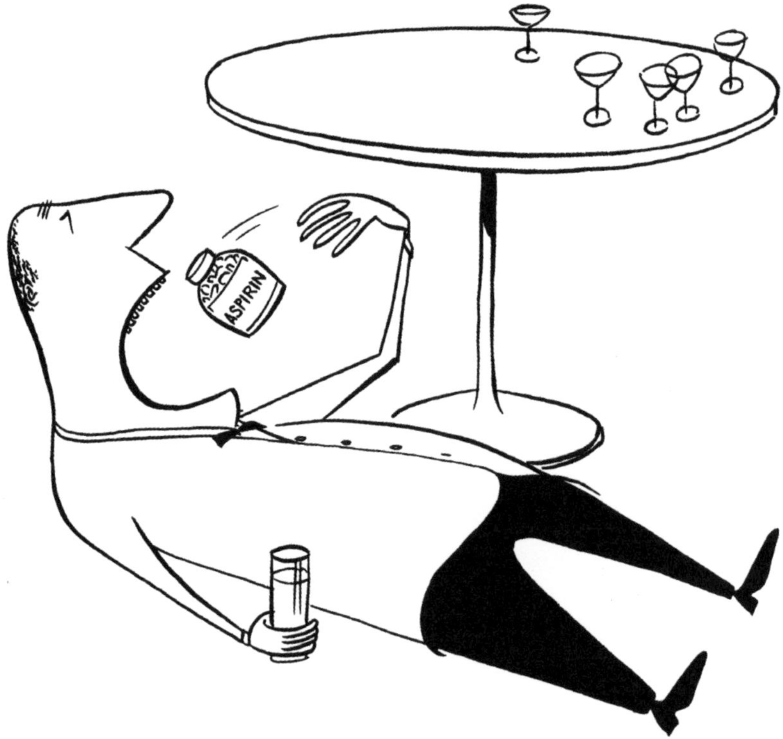
ASPIRIN

The Aspirin Technique

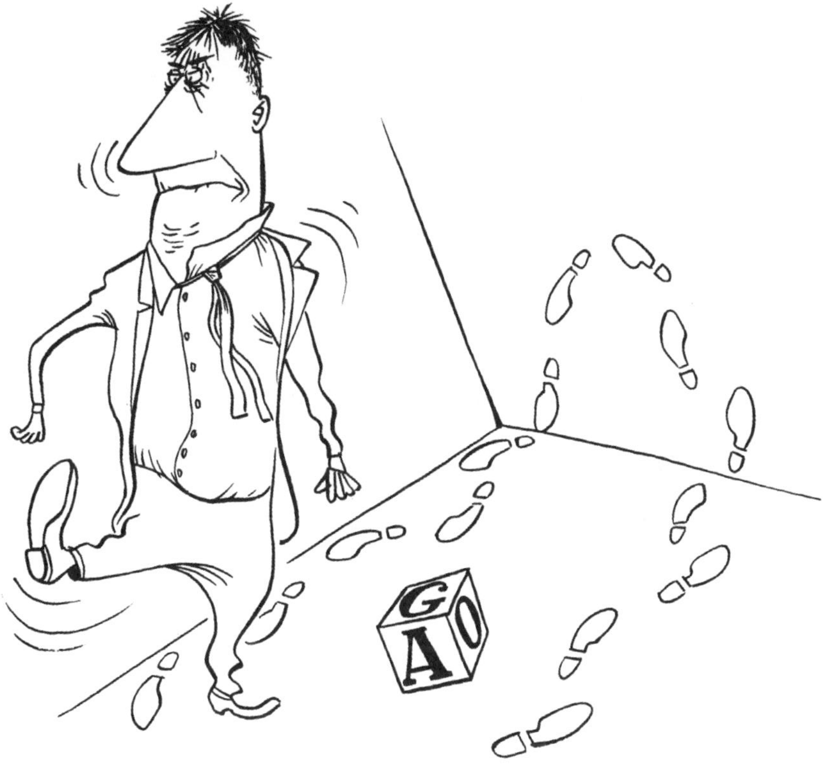
G
A
O

The Walk-Around-the-Block Remedy

VIP views

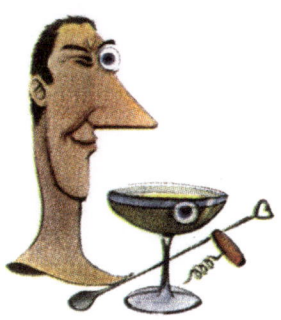

THE DRINK

as seen by...

The Bartender

The Customer

The Wolf

The Wife

The W.C.T.U.

The Old Maid

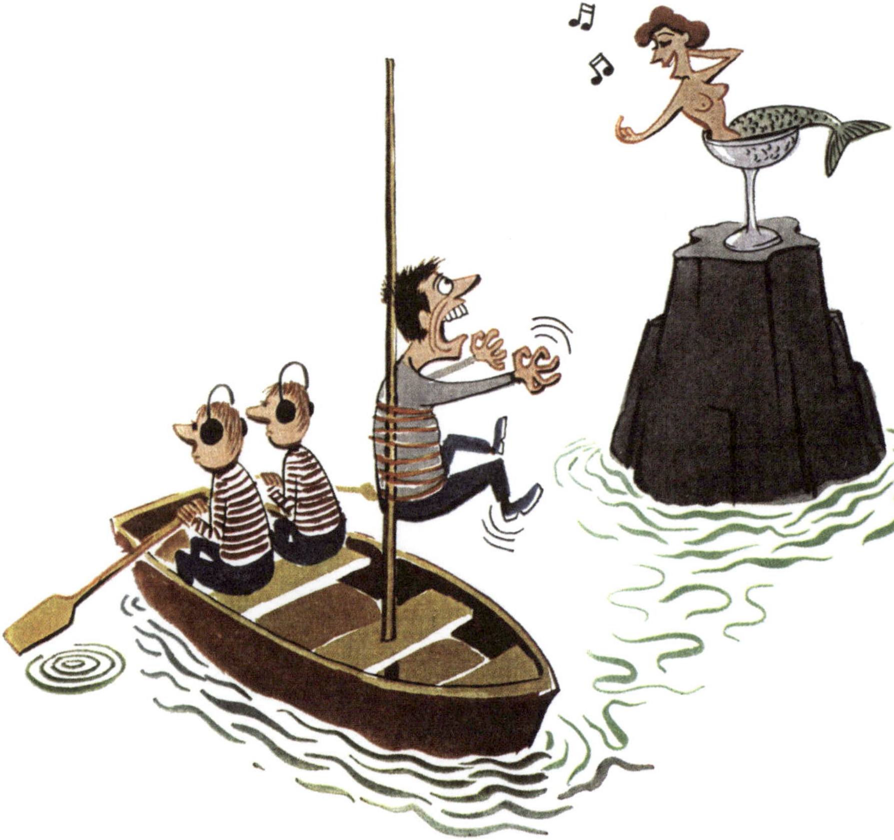

The Guy on the Wagon

DR. FREUD'S COCKTAIL PARTY

Introversion

Passive Submissive

Exhibitionism

Wish Fulfillment　　　　*Envy*

Compulsion

Disassociation

Mother Complex

Herd Instinct

Passive Resistance

Inner Conflict

Hallucinations

Rejection

Schizophrenia

Regression　　　　　*Hostility*

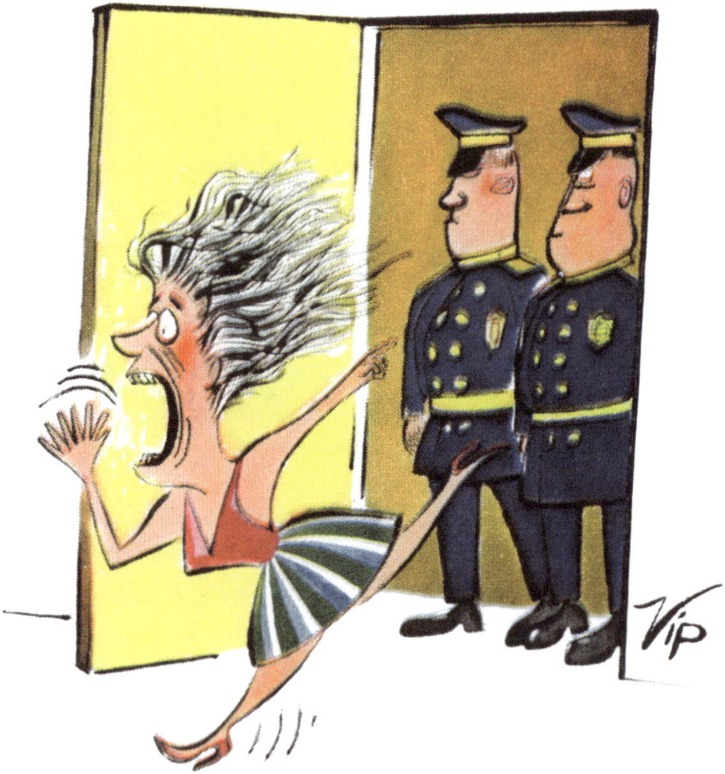
Vip

Hysteria

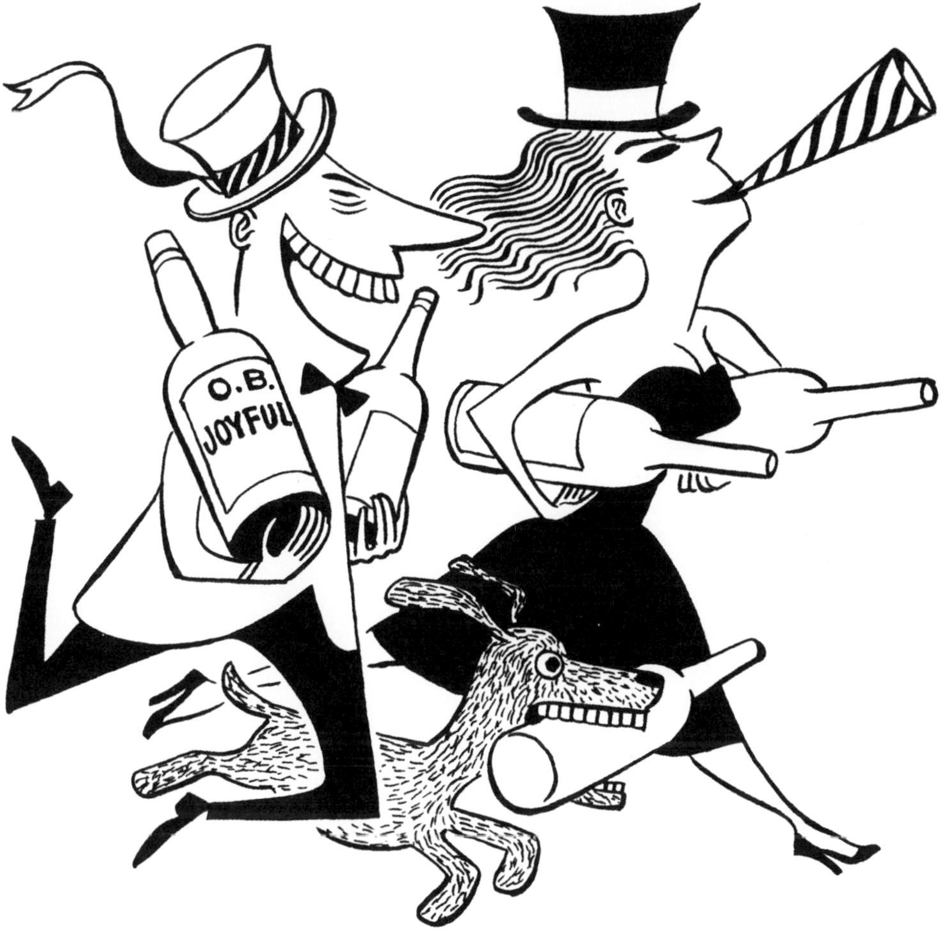
O.B.
JOYFUL

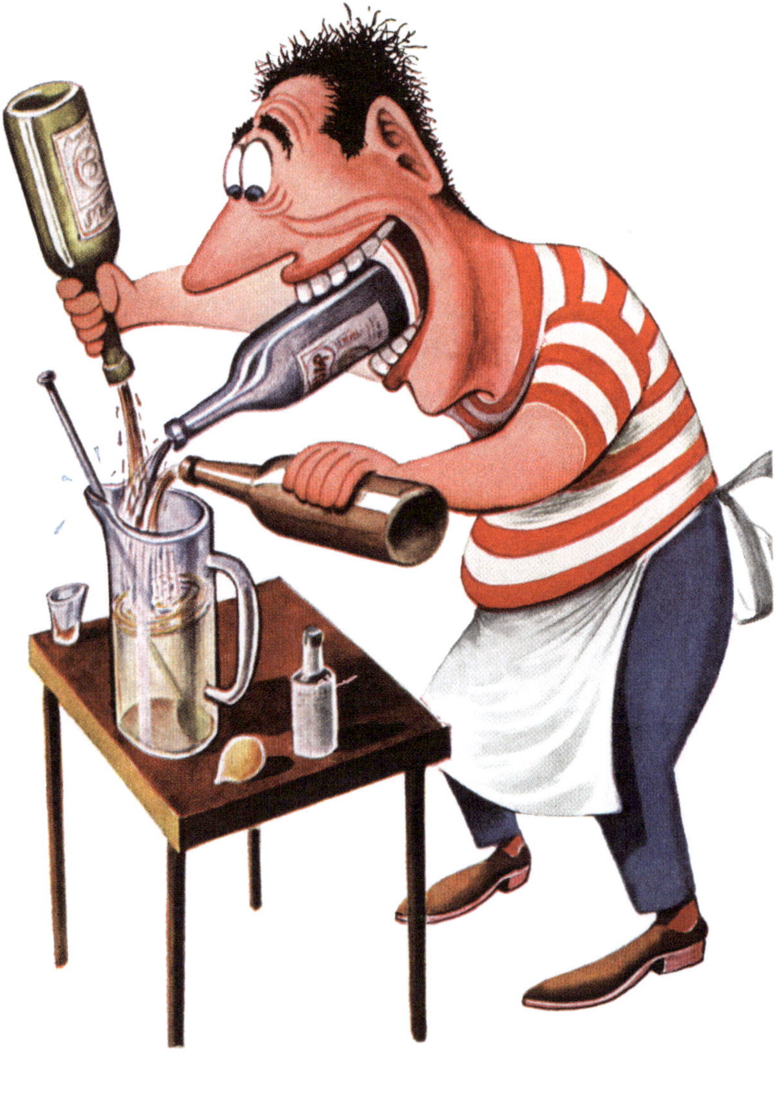

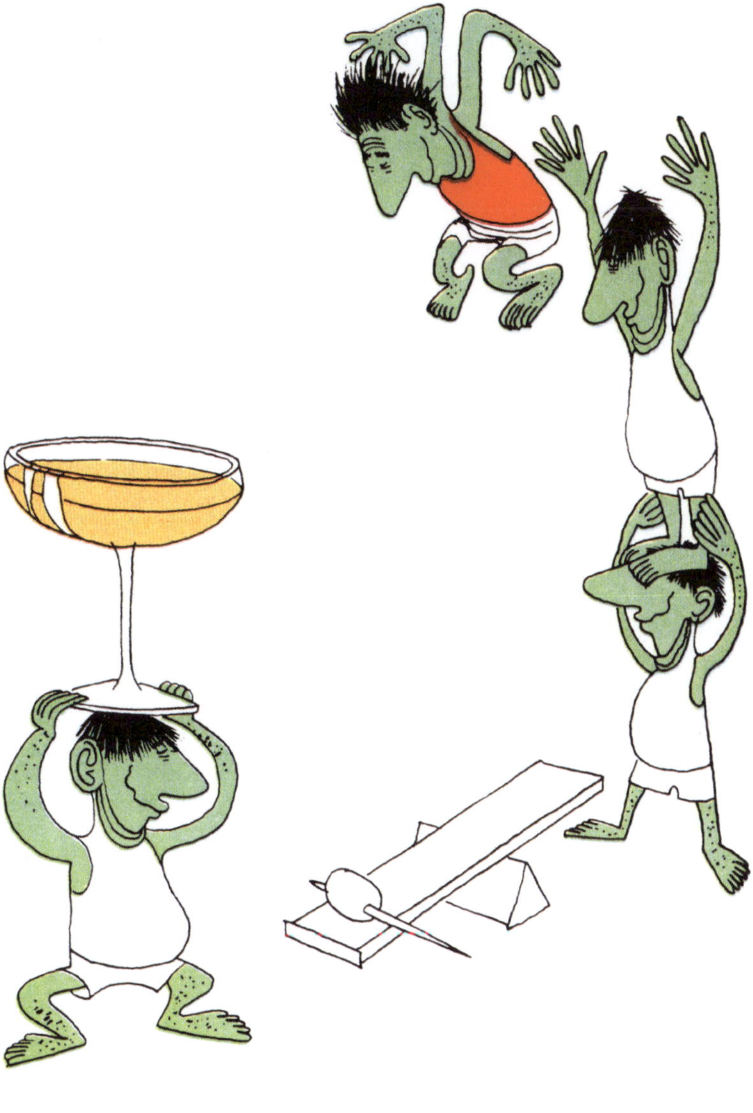

"I take it we're not going out tonight."

"Careful. You know what one Martini does to you."

"Happy birthday to you. Happy birthday to you ..."

"I hope you're not doing all this just because I'm your boss."

"A little something I had left over from the twenties."

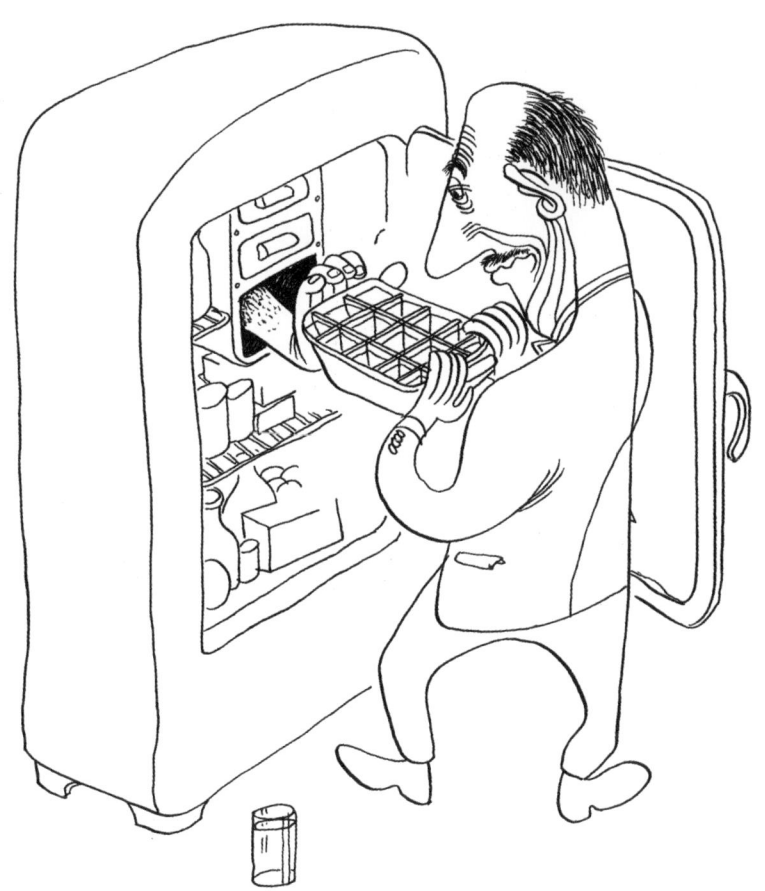

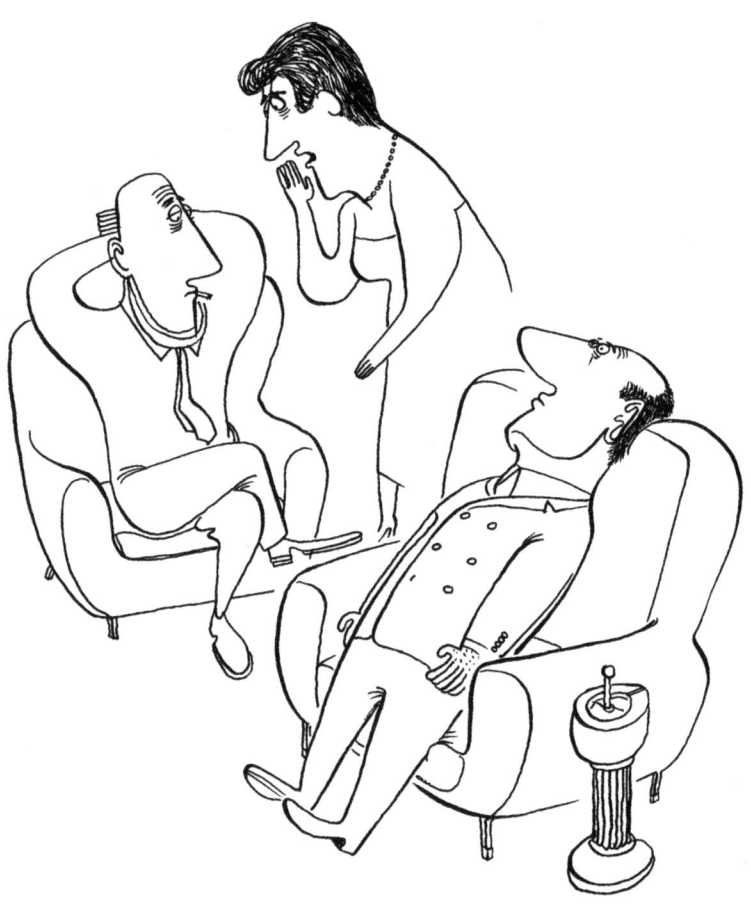

"Maybe he'd feel more at ease with a drink in his hand."

"Honey, Mr. Filstrup's drink is empty again."

"Well, you just go make your eggnogs somewhere else, Buster!"

"It's my birthday. I'll make whiskey sours any place I see fit."

"Look — the first bottle's gone to Ed's head."

"I wouldn't worry. His is just boric acid sollution."

"Gad! All the stores are shut, and we're out of booze!"

"Why didn't you <u>tell</u> me this was going to be a drunken brawl?"

"Just a shade more gin, I think, Hawkins."

"Some people can drink and some can't, I always say."

"Nice going!"

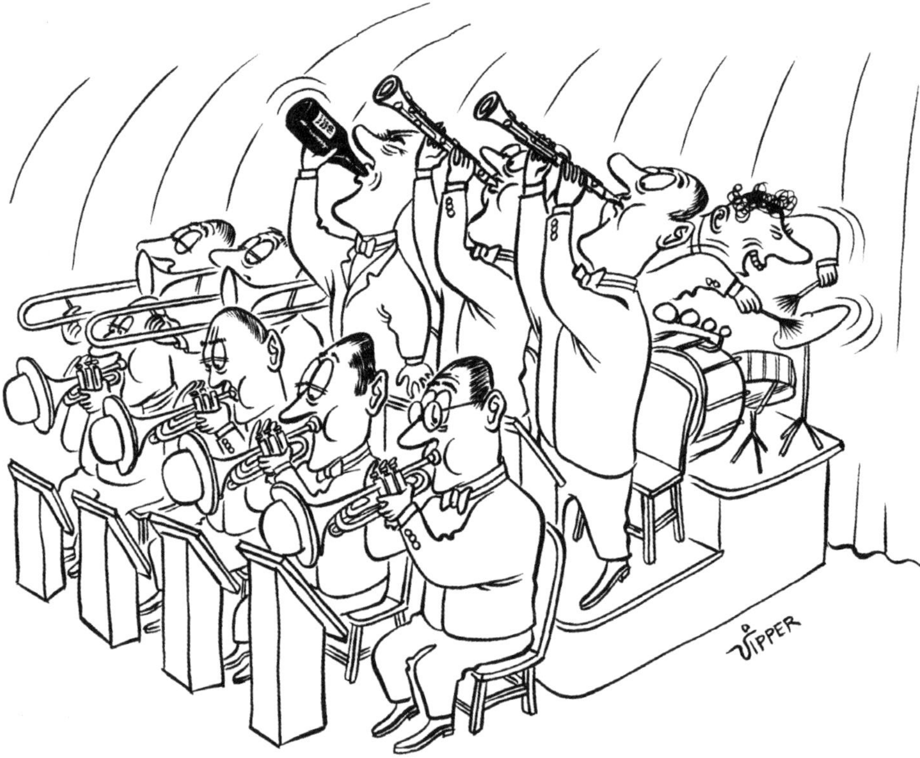
VIPPER

VIP'S TIPS

HOW TO
TAPER OFF...

Put something disagreeable in all your booze.
Something, say, like too much water ...

Keep candy handy. When the urge for a jolt gets overpowering,
be all prepared ... Wife can eat the bonbons.

If it's the company you are keeping, move away.
Where? Where people don't drink ...

*It's easy to stay out of bars. This method is easy
on the willpower, too, but lumber's costly.*

With this type of "shakes" you'll never touch lips to more than a mild spray ... Called "bent-shaft" jitters ...

Or, the way I look at it, all the world hates a quitter, so just drill a hole in your head.

— *Virgil Partch*

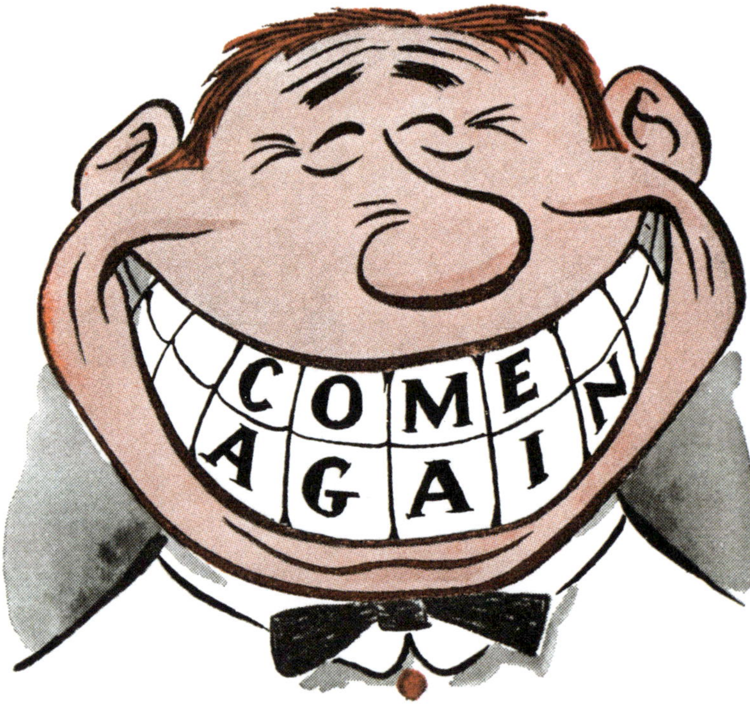
COME
AGAIN